Reptiles

Rod Theodorou

Heinemann LIBRARY

First published in Great Britain by
Heinemann Library,
Halley Court, Jordan Hill, Oxford OX2 8EJ
a division of Reed Educational and Professional
Publishing Ltd.
Heinemann is a registered trademark of Reed
Educational & Professional Publishing Ltd.
OXFORD MELBOURNE AUCKLAND
JOHANNESBURG BLANTYRE GABORONE
IBADAN PORTSMOUTH (NH) USA CHICAGO

Designed by Celia Floyd
Illustrations by Alan Fraser
Printed in Hong Kong/China

03 02 01 00 99
10 9 8 7 6 5 4 3 2 1

ISBN 0 431 03074 X

British Library Cataloguing in Publication Data

Theodorou, Rod
  Reptiles. – (Animal young)
1. Reptiles – Infancy – Juvenile literature
I. Title
597.9'139

Acknowledgements
The Publishers would like to thank the following for
permission to reproduce photographs:

BBC: Michael Pitts p. 6, Martha Holmes p. 7, Tony
Pooley p. 14, Pete Oxford p. 16, Mike Wilkes p. 26;
Bruce Coleman: Jane Burton p. 20; Frank Lane: T
Davidson p. 8, J Louwman p. 18; NHPA: Daniel
Heuclin p. 10, Karl Switak p. 12, B Jones & M
Shimlock p. 17, Rich Kirchner p. 23, Eric Soder p. 25;
OSF: Michael & Patricia Fogden p. 5, Mark Jones p.
9, Maurice Tibbles p. 11, Martin Chillmaid p. 15, Z
Leszczynski pp. 21, 24, M Deeble & V Stone p. 22, Dr
F Koster p. 27; Tony Stone: Stephen Cooper p. 13,
Gary Braasch p. 19.

Cover photograph reproduced with permission of
Animals Animals/Zig Leszcynski

Every effort has been made to contact copyright
holders of any material reproduced in this book.
Any omissions will be rectified in subsequent
printings if notice is given to the Publisher.

Any words appearing in the text in bold, **like this**,
are explained in the Glossary.

Contents

Introduction

There are many different kinds of animals. All animals have babies. They look after their babies in different ways.

These are the six main animal groups.

Mammal   Bird   Reptile

Amphibian   Fish   Insect

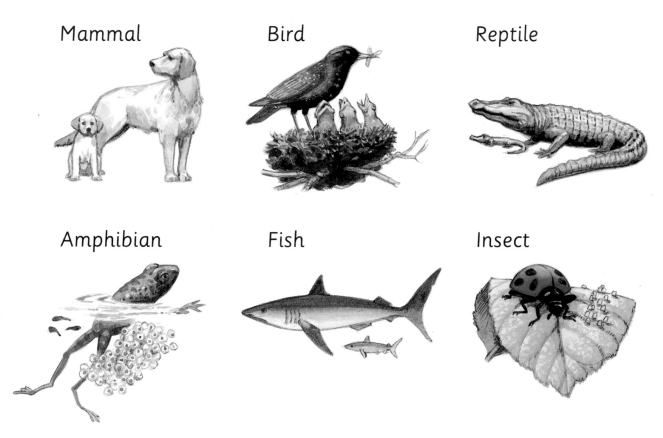

This book is about reptiles. Lizards, snakes, crocodiles, alligators, tortoises and turtles are all reptiles. Most reptiles live in hot places like deserts or rainforests.

This Australian Bearded Lizard lives in the desert.

what is a reptile?

All reptiles:
- breathe air
- are covered in **scaly** skin.

Komodo dragon

Scaly skin

Most reptiles:

- lay eggs on land that **hatch** into babies
- are brightly coloured
- live in hot countries and sunbathe to keep warm.

This marine iguana sunbathes for most of the day.

Building a nest

Most reptiles lay their eggs in a hole in the ground or under a rock. Alligators make a huge nest out of mud and leaves.

Alligators dig a hole in the middle of their nests to lay their eggs in.

8

Turtles spend all their lives in the sea, but they lay their eggs on land. During the night they crawl up a beach and dig a deep hole in the sand to lay their eggs in.

This turtle uses its **flippers** to dig a hole.

Laying eggs

Most reptile eggs are white and soft like paper or **leather**. They are full of **yolk**, just like a bird's egg.

Some lizards and snakes, like this Boa Constrictor, do not lay eggs. Their young are born alive.

Many reptile babies are eaten by **predators**, so mother reptiles lay lots and lots of eggs. This way some of their babies will escape being eaten and grow up.

This green turtle mother can lay up to 200 eggs in one night!

Looking after the eggs

Most reptiles lay their eggs and then leave them. They do not look after them or protect the **hatchlings**. A few reptiles do stay with their eggs.

This python stays with its eggs. It has wrapped itself around them to keep them warm.

Alligators take good care of their nests and eggs.
The mother stands by the nest. She will not eat
for weeks just so she can stay with her eggs.

Alligators will attack any **predators** who
want to steal their eggs.

Hatching eggs

When some baby alligators or crocodiles are ready to **hatch** they start to make grunting sounds inside the egg. The mother hears them and scratches open the nest to help them escape.

This crocodile mother is carefully cracking open her egg with her jaws.

Baby snakes and crocodiles have a special sharp bump called an 'egg-tooth' on their **snouts**. This helps them cut or crack open their egg.

After hatching these baby corn snakes may rest in their broken eggs for hours before they slide off.

Race for the sea

Once turtle mothers have buried their eggs in a hole, they swim away. About six weeks later the eggs **hatch**. Crabs and seabirds gather on the beach to eat the babies.

These baby turtles have to dig their way up through the sand.

The tiny turtles have to crawl as fast as they can to the sea. Even in the sea there may be large fish and hungry sharks waiting to eat them.

Only a few turtles **survive** to grow to be adults.

Live birth

Some reptiles do not lay eggs. Their babies grow inside them and then are born alive.

Some kinds of chameleon lay eggs, others give birth to live young.

When the young are born the mother does not look after them. The babies leave their mother and start to look for food.

This huge anaconda snake can give birth to up to 50 live babies at a time. Each baby is as long as your arm!

Finding food

Reptile parents do not feed their **hatchlings**. The moment the young reptiles are born they have to catch their own food. They eat insects and other small animals.

This young crocodile has caught a fish.

Reptile young are born strong and fast. They can hunt for food just like their parents.

This young copperhead snake's tail looks like a tasty worm. When an animal gets close to eat it, the snake bites and eats the animal.

Looking after the young

Crocodiles and alligators do take good care of their young. The young stay together in groups. The adults watch out for **predators**, like snakes or birds.

Sometimes Nile crocodile mothers carry their babies on their back to keep them safe.

22

Alligator young call out to their parents when they need help. If one of them gets lost it will make a loud call. The large females quickly rush to find it.

Mother alligators will look after their young for up to three years.

Staying safe

Young reptiles are very small. Many other animals hunt and eat them. Most reptiles stay safe by keeping very still, so they are hard to spot, or by quickly running away.

This baby chameleon is smaller than your little finger.

Young lizards can drop their tails if an **enemy** attacks. If a hunter grabs them by the tail, the tail drops off and they escape. A new tail will slowly grow back.

This common wall lizard has dropped its tail.

Growing up

As young reptiles grow they get too big for their skin. They rub against a stone. Their skin splits and comes off, leaving new skin underneath. This is called **shedding**.

This grass snake has shed its skin.

Some reptiles grow quickly. By the time they are one year old, young crocodiles are almost as long as your arm. Newborn tortoises are tiny and grow much slower.

A newborn tortoise is not much bigger than your fist.

Reptiles and other animals

		Fish
What they look like:	Bones inside body	all
	Number of legs	none
	Hair on body	none
	Scaly skin	most
	Wings	none
	Feathers	none
Where they live:	Lives on land	none
	Lives in water	all
How they are born:	Grows babies inside body	some
	Lays eggs	most
How they feed young:	Feeds baby milk	none
	Bring babies food	none

	Amphibians	Insects	Reptiles	Birds	Mammals
	all	none	all	all	all
	4 or none	6	4 or none	2	2 or 4
	none	all	none	none	all
	none	none	all	none	few
	none	most	none	all	some
	none	none	none	all	none
	most	most	most	all	most
	some	some	some	none	some
	few	some	some	none	most
	most	most	most	all	few
	none	none	none	none	all
	none	none	none	most	most

29

Glossary

enemy an animal that will kill another animal for food or for its home

flipper the flat parts of a reptile's body that stick out and are used for swimming

hatch to be born from an egg

hatchling name for a baby when it has just been born from an egg

leather tough and hard animal skin that is used to make shoes, clothes and bags

predator an animal that hunts and kills other animals for food

scaly skin that is covered with small, flat pieces of hard, dry skin

shed to lose an old layer of skin when a new, bigger one has grown

snout a long nose

survive to stay alive

yolk part of an egg that is food for a baby animal

Further reading

Crocodile, Claire Robinson, *Really Wild*, Heinemann Library, 1997.

Prickly and Smooth, Rod Theodorou and Carole Telford, *Animal Opposites*, Heinemann Library, 1996.

Snake and Lizard, Rod Theodorou and Carole Telford, *Spot the Difference*, Heinemann Library, 1996.

Snake, Claire Robinson, *Really Wild*, Heinemann Library, 1999.

The Dorling Kindersley Big Book of Knowledge, Dorling Kindersley, 1994.

The Usborne Book of World Wildlife, Usborne, 1994.

Index